Silence of Islands

poems

W. M. Raebeck

cover painting by Charles Raebeck (his one painting in 95 years)
cover design, interior drawings by W. M. Raebeck

Library of Congress Control Number: 2020936873

ISBN 978-1-938691-15-7

30% of the proceeds from this book goes to protecting wilderness, wildlife, all creatures and oceans from human violation, insensitivity, and ignorance.

This book is sourced from a responsibly managed North American forest, meeting the requirements of the Independent Sustainable Forestry Initiative Program.® W. M. Raebeck lives in a zero waste household and believes living simply, curtailing waste, and consuming less will save our planet.

W. M. Raebeck books are available in paperback and ebook from all booksellers, book stores and libraries. (Place order if not available.) You can also email Hula Cat Press for orders, questions, and info.

WendyRaebeck.com has books, promotions, and sign-ups for newsletter. Other books by author listed on last page of this book.

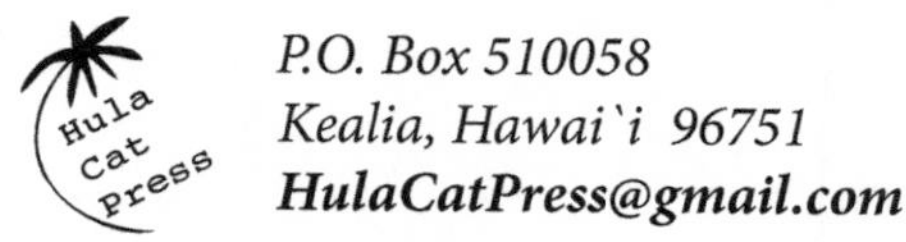

P.O. Box 510058
Kealia, Hawai'i 96751
HulaCatPress@gmail.com

— to my parents —

Charles Raebeck
and
Charlotte Heider Raebeck

with their brilliant minds
and humor that rolled in like the waves

to fulfill your dreams
is my dream

Acknowledgements

Compiling decades of poetry was a bigger undertaking than I reckoned. I didn't factor in the emotion, even the pain, of revisiting delicate issues again and again with every edit. Practically wore me out. I'd be thinking, "This poem is so freakin' sad, nobody should read this," or "I can't confess this — no one else has ever been so foolish or naive," or "I love this one, but would normal people?"

My uncertainties were quelled by three separate editors over a period of about six years — Marcie Powers, Donna Carsten, and Anndrias Hardisty. From their feedback, I was able to select, groom, and organize the final collection you're wading into. I can't thank them enough for their honesty, care, and support.

Since I'd instructed them not to sugar-coat their commentary, I expected tougher task-masters. And had they said, "Stick to memoir, kid," I'd have packed up this pile o' poems without a sniffle. Instead, they encouraged me, saying my verses made their own feelings less isolated and obtuse; ease in reading made 'poetry' more invitational than they expected; and my realness let them trust me. And they felt the female heart was revealed truthfully here.

So sincere thanks to Marcie, Donna, and Anndrias for their time, care, and counsel.

I also have to acknowledge — because there's so much damn love in this book — my romantic partners (reflecting an era of freedom and the power of love and attraction). My acting teacher, Elizabeth Dillon, used to say, "When you fall in love, you learn to sing. And when you lose your love, you really learn to sing." So it goes for poetry. So I thank all who've entered my heart.

Now over to you. May you find solace and lightness here, memory and emotion.

Thank you for reading.

— *WMR*

Notes

Should you wonder why there are 'father' poems but not 'mother' poems, it's because my mother passed away in 1969 (at only age 45), thus Dad was my only parent for nearly fifty years. But my mother's spirit is far from absent.

'Amagansett,' frequently mentioned, is my hometown, a hamlet in the Town of East Hampton on eastern Long Island. 'Zaxos,' is a fictional name given to a Greek island in the Aegean.

Regarding sequencing, though all the poems have dates, they're not chronologically presented. I strove for flow and tempo rather than historical order. And it probably goes without saying that arranging the succession of this many poems is no minor task. 'Herding cats' is an apt metaphor.

Silence of Islands

Contents

Part 1

Part II

Part III

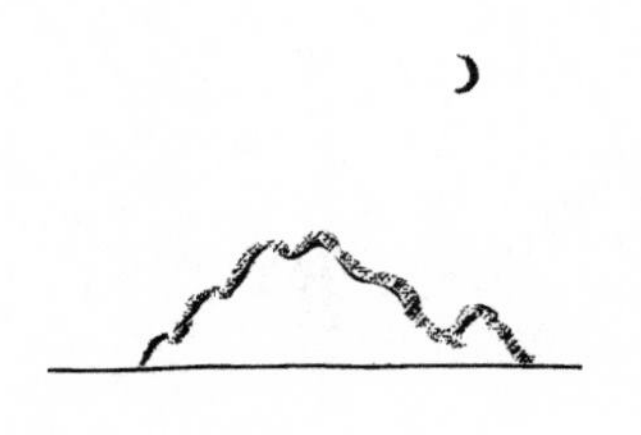

Part 1

Poetic License

There's a little office
where you get your poetic license –
every state has one
a government agency
but you have to be tipped off
you can't Google the location

And you have to crawl there
have to arrive with bloody hands and knees
have to be in tears
your clothes filthy
pockets empty

But if you show up
on a certain day
like the 11th or the 21st of each month
they're open
And there's a password
to punch in

but there's an element of sheer luck
when you tap it in
Hopefully the door clicks open
because even though you crawled there
on your hands and knees
you have to deserve it

You don't have to write a poem
to get a poetic license
or ten poems or twenty
You have to know poetry –
sentence fragments
non-structure
words that erupt from the innards
and the passing of time
where the ticking is so thunderous
and frightening
you're up all night

You have to know the ocean isn't only
for swimming
but an emotional being wrangling with the shore
you have to know that 'nothing'
the word 'nothing'
is so loaded
so comprehensive
that it has the wrong definition in the dictionary

These are some criteria
for getting your license
and the only way they can be put into words
is through a poem

At the office
they're not overflowing with congratulation
they're doing business
but they're nice
have knowing eyes
and their few questions are thought provoking
So you hand them the fee
which is nominal
and you can top off the tip jar
for the next poet

And when you turn to go
they wish you well

At some point
they'll send your license
But just by going there
you know you got it
And it can't be revoked

The vast majority of your countrymen
don't even know about the poetic licensing agency
but don't let that impede you
Write often and well
let it rip, stand tall
edit more often and better
and I'll see you
where the waves meet the shore

November 27, 2017, Kaua'i

White Cat Sleeping
in the Moonlight

sometimes we're determined to suffer
sometimes things are so good they're bad
sometimes 'I don't know' is a monster,
even where dreams have come true
there's a void

God's gone fishin'
nobody's home
not even me
just a white cat sleeping in the moonlight

but the lemon tree's thick with fruit
the breeze so sweet it drowns you
the night so safe
the life so long
the luck so vast
there aren't words or prayers
just a white cat sleeping in the moonlight

July 21, 2019, Wailua, Kaua'i

Better Them than Us

My blue shirt
lying on top of your green hooded sweater
has a new feeling about it
The two have been heaped on a pile of blankets
for ten days now
But before, the green sweater was just a hostage
made me annoyed in fact that you'd forgotten it
This time you asked if you could leave it
for future beach walks
It's the first time any of your stuff
has gotten mixed in with my stuff
and I like the way it looks
In fact I think my blue shirt
is in love with your green sweater

March 17, 1985, Venice Beach

No Story Here

I could smoke a pack of Camels right now
and not even cough
I'm so inured to stuff I don't even like
It's past the seven suicidal years
It's past 5 o'clock
yet it's taken all day just to sit down
and now it's time to leave

When there's time I don't have any
when there's none I find some
I wish I could go sit on a rock somewhere

I'd make a great peasant
a great pauper
with a few chickens and one old goat
I'd write great stories then

September 2, 1976, Amagansett

Truces

A hole in the clouds
I needed
I was a pin cushion
without room for one more pin
a used-up voodoo doll
nothing going through me but needles
Still I believed. Magic was, even though I wasn't
Magic is
But I was twisted like a cop's doughnut
an Alpine road
a fundamentalist mind
Tomorrow just left
Yesterday was hanging around
like a drunk Indian

A drunk Indian was hanging around
in Santa Fe
and I was walking by looking for Magic
A nickel, a quarter, a penny –
I drew from my pocket
one by one. Another penny.
"I think there's more," I said, stalling for time
because I wanted another look into his eyes
He was so straight – green-eyed Indian
with black ponytail
and red face from the beer

Right there on the edge between young and old
I couldn't not see him, or pass his power
The power of his birthright stared in my eyes
I handed him the coins
The corner dropped away, and Santa Fe with it –
all the parading yuppies
adobe colors against the gray day remained
and we started talking about land

Talking about land with an American Indian,
I realized,
was what I'd wanted to do all my life
We talked all afternoon,
climbed a hill, took pictures of each other
He took out his ponytail for the camera
and his thick black hair
almost reached his handmade belt
He lives alone way up in the mountains
in a teepee
A family of mountain lions are his friends
He carries bones from Safeway
up the mountain for them
He won't look at white people

In a dead Indian these ways
are considered awesome to the white;
In a live Indian, it's "homelessness"

"Talk to me a little more," I said,
"before I go back to my life."
"About what?"
"The mountains, what you know.
Give me some of your purity
to take with me. I need it."
And he told me more of the sweetness,
the goodness of the Earth
Talked about the sky in Chiricahua
his native tongue
then translated for me
He needed me, too
I cried for my ancestral sins against his people
I couldn't help it –
looking into that obliterated power

But Magic is
Magic swirled around and through us
We both became better people
finding ourselves again in another race
another angle of humanity
The Indian in me was crying
the White Man in him was crying
and it started to rain.
Arms around each other
under an adobe ledge
we made a truce

April 8, 1990, in flight, Albuquerque to LA

The Spider

*They call this darkness
here where the spider died
Chasing him with the broom
I meant no harm.
I thought he was faking that limp
as he struggled to scream
I thought he was playing dead like a pill bug
when he lay on his back
but I became more gentle then
and laid him on a little bed of straw
only to witness his final effort.
Looking to the sky that was bright blue then
I muttered my apologies
and said stupidly that maybe here on the straw
one of his own kind would rescue him
Sure
Maybe they would bring a first aid kit
an ambulance*

*Again I try to be clever
while my innocent fellow,
no tarantula, no black widow, no threat at all
especially now –
lies lifeless where I landed him
I'm just a bumbling human, I meant no harm*

September 4, 1975, Zaxos, Greece

This Empty Beach

This empty beach
is so full
it floods my heart

the sand is cold
the big waves sound like freight trains
everything's gray and white and strong

the wave of my soul
was born on this beach
I was seven years old when I stepped into
these sand slippers

hours, days, months, years
decades
we rolled in this warmth
Mom watched us
in our red bathing suits
"stay in front of the lifeguard stand"
We'd look back from the waves
and see her round dark glasses

Dad and Mom
the huge blanket
no food, no drink, no towels, no shoes
just us
all day every day

all summer, every summer
riding waves till we were freezing
then lying in the sand
till we were burning
repeat

the beach has endured
the lack of change is stunning
our sandy gang
has dispersed
Atlanta, New Zealand, heaven
and I'm still here
with Dad, and tears

yet...it's a glorious day
In spirit, heaven is closer
than New Zealand
And there is hope
and time for forgiveness
there are more summers

the waves tell their secrets
to the beach grass
I'm listening:
"Death isn't sad
sadness is death
come and play"

June 5, 2002, Amagansett

Eternity Train

Scoop me up, God
hold me tight tonight
free me
to ride with you
on the gratitude train
the eternity train
the coincidental carousel
the timeless, mindless magic carpet
where emotion, fact and fantasy
are all the same
the feast where the plates are empty
the fast where the soul is full
the promontory above all else
the immaterial value
the space between details
the distance of stars

where the night itself
provides answers
as simple as the rush of the wind
the upward corners of the mouth

May 23, 2015, Kalihiwai, Kaua'i

Drink Deep

Drink deep from sorrow's well
once or twice in this life

to be humbled
to draw from pain, as it ebbs

it's okay to be sad
it's beautiful to feel

go into the deepest corner
of your heart
where you almost never go

to love deeply is to be free
willing to hurt
unafraid
unable not to love

it's honest to need

Drink deep from sorrow's well
once or twice in this life

Spring 1975

Stealing You

braided bell ropes
hang at rest
one more red day
sinks to the west
now just a thread
sewn into night
to which most boats
are tied on tight

village lights spill yellow
in lines across the bay
where a single hollow fog horn
is rolling you away
up from the rocky hillside
flies a crooked little moon
that silhouettes a single ship
that stole away too soon

October 1972, Zaxos, Greece

Eat Fish Sleep With

Then you left
You had to,
I guess
I found new ones
to eat, fish, sleep with....
drink with
fish with...
sleep fish eat with
fish eat sleep
drink fish sleep eat fish sleep drink eat
sleep fish drink eat fish sleep eat drink

And when we eat drink sleep without you
and when we fish
when we fish
I wish...
if only you...
But you had to leave
I guess

September 1974, Zaxos, Greece

Again, Two Years Later

Sound of color of sound
the drumming of hooves on stone
and high shepherd cries freely fly
down the stream of goat bells
where silver sings sounds of lucid blue
Oh, I long to wake you
just to say good morning

Morning
Farther away the mules bray
from the throes of love, orgasmically
and the bells trickle now more quietly
like a breeze through feathered trees
holding a hill shade still
while your even breathing swings me
in its hammock
your brown leg warm across mine

Time
keeps her loves like treasures
which she hides for us to find
and sleep beside
in the striped blue and white Greek night
where our senses swim
unwound in sound
moist melons of sound
cool and swollen round
with taste – peponi, karpoozi –
found
one of time's pink hidden seashells
and the smell of salt

The sliding of ships won't wake you
nor the silence of islands
nor the shadows that surface
your slumbering haze
nor my soft muslin gaze
But wild, a child, still I creep, barefoot
to peek at your sleep
afraid to stir your tranquil shade

Goddess of Time
in her white stone rooms of years
stands golden in a gown of hours
that want to cling,
but seduced by time and the wind
opens blue-green windows instead
through which days have fled
And flowered moments still blooming behind us
are again in season, want to find us
your song-like sleep, my quiet wait
hold the eye of a second
an even escape
from the easy rhyme of wing-ed time

And the three windmills that crown the hill
turn counter the clock now
and hold her still
And for the breath of a second,
just the breath of one second,
time was perfectly, perfectly still

July 1974, Zaxos, Greece

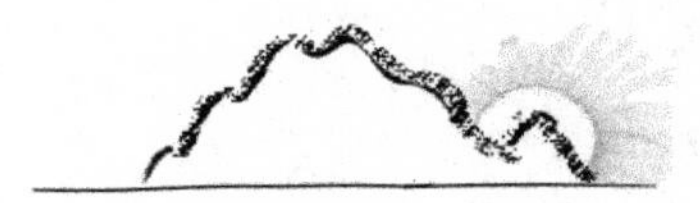

Be Greedy

Stay well
to suck the juice out of life
be selfish
about health
grab it greedily

Health is the only place
greed is respected
so grab all you can
of knowledge and of practice
grab for dear life

January 31, 2020, Wailua, Kaua'i

Love we Want

"Just because I don't love you the way you want,"
Dad once told me
"doesn't mean I don't love you"
It was a lesson
about all love
about expectation
and acceptance

The love we get
may not be what we think we need
but maybe Someone else
knows more about our needs

May 29, 2002, Bridgehampton

Close Friends

I met an Englishman in London
named Max.
I married him
so he could live with me in New York.
A Greek friend of his, George,
also married an American
so he could live with her in New York.
Another Greek friend of Max and George, Yanni,
married an English ballerina
so he could live with her in London;
then they moved to New York.
To stay there,
they had to divorce and each marry an American.

A few years later,
I met another Englishman in LA
I wanted to marry him
(even though I already had my English visa).
Max agreed to divorce,
so I wouldn't be heir to his new business partnership.

One New York afternoon,
Max and I were divorced uptown
by a lawyer friend.
At the same moment, downtown,
Yanni married Josie, Max's partner
(becoming heir to the business).
Yanni's ballerina
married a gay guy from Pittsburg
to convince his family he was straight,
then her American dance company moved
to Europe.
In Athens, she ran into George.
They fell in love, went to Rome,
and were married
in a taxi by a Franciscan monk
(both becoming bigamists).
Yanni had an affair with Max's new girlfriend.
My new boyfriend
had an affair with my girlfriend.
George and the ballerina
came back to visit their friends.
And George's first wife
married the lawyer who divorced Max and me.

July 10, 1982, London

Behind the Mime

*Pink clouds are stacking up above the sunset
roller skaters fight the wind
performers fold and pack their props
Where will the mime go?*

*Behind the gilded palms I search the chilly crowd
for that lonely pride*

*There's no end to this flock of seagulls
they pour out of a broken cloud somewhere
Is that where the mime lives now?
He asked for everything and I said yes –
averting my eyes from the jars of white-face,
the stuffed rabbit he unpacked
Leg-warmers were about all I could swallow
Just be quiet about your work, I thought
No, no, be anything but quiet!
Don't be a mime*

*The crowd thins. The mime never walks by.
In some garage or basement or anti-space
he's playing with illusion, mirrors
and side-stepping...
asking for nothing
except all you can possibly give*

I offered less than he needed
and he was stricken with pantomime grief
Less than all? No house, no food,
no shelf for my leotards?
No mirror in which to shave my head?
Kisses and care and company,
I shrunk in saying

He puffed up as he shook his head
then lifted off – as though attached to balloons
With almost a frown he insisted life is a dance
As for a partner, he has a mirror

The clouds are mauve and thinning
The mime won't come, or phone
or toy with the thought
Our curtain came down too soon
so he's returned to the bleak anti-love
that he cultivates for insight
My compassion is no umbrella for the rain
so he doubles his silence until I fade

February 3, 1985, Venice

NYC Nights

Men sit in night New York lofts
and the rain pours down in open windows
Men discuss space and history
find friendship in cognac
I'm a woman and I'm in love
Men go on and on
With words they'll figure out science
and the universe
with music they'll travel
where their feet won't go
I cook the food
I want to

The night gets deep
I want a different fulfillment
I wait
Men know how to wait, I keep learning
Men know time
For me it comes and goes
like a meal, like weather
Men have a constancy, a continuation
I come and go, a tide

I am a woman, corny, a cliché
When I'm in love there is only that
my melancholia a river
my complaints expressible
my dissatisfaction close at hand

I can't smoke and drink
I try but am not made to
I'm supposed to be a cloud
but can't find my sky
I'm supposed to be radiant, can't find my sun
Supposed to be a laugh
can't find the tease

Men without women wish silently
Continuity pulls them to a new morning
Continuity circles back for me
in a sleepless night,
learning to wait
I'm in love and I have to wait

Trying to be a man doesn't come easy
for a woman
measuring right and wrong
against anybody's guess
Late at night
in August rain with mutual cognac
life divides and I want the female side
the weary yawn, the nightgown
soft pillows in a clean bed

I don't want black holes and cigarettes
I don't want more music, more coffee
after midnight
I want to be with the dawn
the running water
the sun at daybreak, a light in the eye
a reason for someone to wake up

August 11, 1979, NYC

Right

What does 'right' mean?
we all think we're right
but who's right when an old man's heart
is broken

The art beyond right
and wrong
is love

'no blame'
goes a long way

seeing an old man cry
breaks my heart too
In the universe
of this family
he's our creator

and while we have breath
let us make amends

May 29, 2002, Bridgehampton

Somewhere

Sittin' on a bench, somewhere in the universe
the planet glides through the galaxy
the mountains are obscured by smog
and I'm tempted to move on

only tempted
a seedling in a glass of water,
I've grown a root
my past has been erased
the word 'future' extracted from the dictionary
like an aching molar
Near forty
I make a list of all I need to unlearn
to seek a new way

But my abilities smolder like a fire at two a.m.
after everyone's gone to bed
Like pins at the end of a bowling lane
they refuse me a strike
My certainties bring uneasiness now
not calm
my wisdom brings angst
not confidence

my secret disappointments
however universal
have a finality that forbids one more
My architectural mind
my personal Eiffel Tower
is in some nondescript skyline
not even in Paris

I'm destined to an eternity
of gazing out the window
of a twelfth grade classroom
wondering what I'll be

The underside of earthly living
seems so ordinary, so lazy
the topside so untouched...

March 14, 1989, Venice

Striped Shorts

It's not too late
It's never too late
for life

Start all over
start from scratch
break the mold
forget the past, the present
and the future –
that imaginary future
we kowtow to

Forget health and death and age
structure and achievement
Forget hanging on, holding on
And wonder who you can become
the one you've always been
the one you've almost been
or occasionally lit upon
in a lost season

Don't think too hard
just release
like a slow sigh
on a summer vacation
in Amagansett

at age ten
the year of the striped shorts
and big bicycle
the onset of freedom

Still being a kid
but feeling taller
mobile and solo
having a secret life
finding stuff
seeing stuff
checking things out
in loose clothes

Like springtime, there was lightness
Saturday was good
Goodness was obvious and everywhere
nature was in us
nothing was illegal
dogs were normal
kids got spanked
You could go anywhere, park anywhere
say anything
Bad manners were the big crime

Everyone had a mother and father
and a house and yard
take-out didn't exist
or Styrofoam

a picnic with hot-dogs and hamburgers
was the fun thing
roasting marshmallows
the best

The year of the striped shorts
can be this year
get a pair
wear 'em out
get a big bike
and check things out
in Amagansett
take a long sigh
and a summer vacation

It's still me
that same kid
on that same beach
lying in the sand with no towel
thinkin' things over
and making a plan
I've survived six times ten years
the future came and went
but the waves never stopped once
the sand never blew away

June 2, 2011, Coastguard Beach, Amagansett

Country

I see my country goin' city
I see my corn growin' gritty
trucks ridin' my lane
makin' me insane
I see my country goin' city

I'm watchin' my town turnin' city
watchin' what used to be pretty
my road they's gonna pave
they's a-diggin' my grave
I see my town turnin' city

I can't quit this ol' town turnin' city
guess I'll let my ol' corn get gritty
they can lock up my room
I'll be a-dyin' soon
I see my country goin' city

August 1969, Amagansett

Undressed

Through the drain of the imagination
seeped the blood
of the early twenties
the early evenings
The mirage of professionalism
crawled from the mountaintop castle
down the rugged crags
to choke on the beach
of skeletal creation
And the poet born to die
undressed for dead
burying his Esperanto
in a prayer for a virgin page

In the longing for meaningful loneliness
and worn by the weather of words
he ravaged the mind's dictionary –
past usefulness and uselessness
past absurdity, silence, objectivity, mirth,
meditation, novelty, love, solitude, God,
intrigue, distraction, despair, and longing

Left with hope, fear, and the sport of clairvoyance,
he faltered, fumbled, and juggled his own words
but dared not disturb the pen
or the night that seemed to continue

Left with continuation
he let a curtain drop
over previous curtains
for no definitive reason

Abandoning the tools of technique,
he became a finger in the sand
writing against the wind,
he became hands with holes
cupping floods of desire,
he became an unstructured abode
housing nothing that held

Playing Russian roulette
with the eight parts of speech,
he murdered the noun
then in a frenzy
obliterated his native tongue
then philosophy, science and religion

Until he was left with only dumbness
mathematics
animals
and a small circle of young children

August 31, 1975, Zaxos, Greece

The Lifeguard

The wind is whipping
beach-goers endure
  keep on sunbathing, playing
  jumping waves, shooting videos
Sailboats bend in the white light on the water
  the air is misty and bright
  children roll in the warm sand

The lifeguard wears his red jacket
  stands in the shoreline
  where the kids are out too deep
Memorial Day weekend – lifeguard's busy
  eyes glued to frolicking figures
  tumbling through waves
  few with competence

A long day for the lifeguard
who began at eight
He strolls back to his tower
face obscured by sunglasses
and straw hat
In an instant he could be back in the water
pulling in a child
or grown-up
who might say thanks
or might be embarrassed
The lifeguard will just go back to work
training his eyes again on the sea

It's four o'clock, but he'll work till six or seven
overtime
Tired, his eyes are sunburned
been a long day
And last night was a long night
making love with me

May 25, 1997, Venice

Half Moon High

Half moon high
late day lets you slide
into my eye
a special time
the sheep bound down
the trees just breathe
the sea washes boats to the beach

you come sailing to my mind
I let you in
your hair on fire tells its wind
and your eyes a-glaze
make me envy where you've been
riding the sea again
your manhood blazing there
rough and windblown
a wave you are

*As island outlines unravel the night
you sleep, eyes open, so as not to die
I never sleep when by your side*

*I like you now as night steals day –
and hope has a fragrant essence
ever concealed in your presence*

*You're a rocky man throwing words like stones
and I'm the climber who seeks your peace
to sit beside
in the evening lavender after your ride*

*I'll tell you a dream I had:
I let the twilight silence your words
and give me your eyes instead
then without a backward glance
we rose together in single trance
and followed an aqua scent
to where mountains laughed
and half hours passed
and kissing was done with the hands*

Now the sun is low, half the moon aglow
your moment is growing old
the sea's translucent gray, like the sky
as ocean horizons, they close,
over which I've peeked
for thoughts of you
your currents and your prose

And I'm island bound in close contour
your blue boat not as blue as before
so I'll let it sail
from my dusky mind
But tomorrow this time
when the shadows spill
I'll meet you again
on this purple hill
where I practice being alone

August 1974, Zaxos, Greece

Boats

the tourist boats, like eggshells, seem fragile,
patched, exhausted in an innocent way
like Kalliopi
whose etched, chiseled face may break
with the withering of her hands
if they wash many more sheets
for the beds of the man-eating traveler

Kalliopi's hands cannot cut many more tomatoes
but she reads the ships like counting coins
her well-being depending
on how heavily they sit
upon the harbor
that once held only fishing boats
like the little green one
a fisherman named after his radiant young wife
Kalliopi

September 2, 1975, Zaxos, Greece

-riend End

They surround you
they laugh
and then they're gone
like a brilliant sunset closing into night

Did they love you?
maybe
Did they judge you?
with certainty
Are they gone forever?
they are

They lost the meaning
lost the 'us'
they went away
still laughing
but 'we' no longer matter

One-sided perspective
they changed their minds
in cold blood
unspoken goodbye –
they even say 'I love you'

The fault is
yours
Go think about it
for years to come
They will not

March 25, 2017, Kaua'i

Please

you don't owe me anything
not babies, not love
I'm not yours, you're not mine
we never made promises
so leave me alone in my pain

don't leave me alone in this pain

I don't know why I'm bound to you
why I can't stop crying
I don't want to want you
trying to learn how not to
but don't think about me because I feel it

please don't stop thinking about me

I'm cracking and breaking
I'll never find you again
my guts and heart are gone, and my brain
and still you only phone
don't phone me anymore

phone me now

I'm waiting for forever without you to begin
you'll never be good to me
time makes it worse
and proximity's a game
you don't love me

please stop loving me

your face is blank
your body is gray
I hardly exist at all
you're just the sound of a car I listen for
don't help me anymore

help me now

you'll never be what I need
you're hours and days too late
this has to be the finale
I'm too weak, I'm too weak
just leave me forever

please don't leave me

October 27, 1980, London

The White House

Morning too full, too beautiful
and evening too peaceful
complaints too few
figs hanging ripe in my trees, too fine
time too significant
time keeps time

And his eyes are so Aegean that I
want to skin-dive there
but cannot for fear
surely I would drown
Adonis is too Greek, too crazy, and too young
and I don't dare
imagine what we might share

Then chaos appeared
– a wicked storm
set fire to the sea
as the fishermen waited
with ouzo for company

I still wanted to stay
even after the wind
took my innocence away
So I untied my books and pen
and through the days I'd swim
I stopped watching the windowed sea
for that boat I knew instantly

Then he came to me in the whiteness of day
with that warm smell of salt
that I thought I forgot
and paraded me in the evening refrain
saying find a house that we can stay in

Long days I searched –
for sacred quiet and fertile earth
and finally saw it, tucked white into a hill
inhaling the view, it was totally still

But it reminded him of another time
when in this same house he had stayed
fires had scorched him deep and black,
and memories shouted "never go back"

Now it wasn't the white house
that burned but me
so I withdrew clandestinely
and sealed my lips
since everyone sees the smoke
coiling where a weak woman spoke
To the village I went only for food
and to the beach for afternoon sleep

Finally Adonis climbed the morning hill,
but only halfway to give a yell
that found me lost in thought
so his echo returned
and he went back down

But the village then beckoned me
with food and wine
so I followed the stones past the setting sun
Ready for words after being enclosed
many and pleasant were the evening hellos
and it was Adonis who passed me the wine
and cool lips tasted fresh figs on mine
he smelled in my hair the cool white stone
and saw in my face what the house had done
"I will come," he said, "I will come"

Summer 1974, Zaxos, Greece

Shaming Them

Leave the zoo and set the lions free
can't you see their eyes?
I shrink before their highness

People laugh at the monkeys
but I can no longer watch
the humans

September 1975, Egypt

To Charlie, Audrey, and the Clan

Though I grow older
and 'home' has many faces
and new places,
the original and the deepest and the dearest
remains with you

Though I race through the hours
of getting here then being here,
though 'here' scatters around me and multiplies
and slips through my hands
with the few precious days
then the last precious hours
until I'm airborne for another home,
my heart overflows with love for this one
for these people
from this fertile soil
where my roots are always nourished

Though I never give enough
and my offerings are as meager as
the simple hope to just be loved
you make it seem that to give to me
is all you want from me
and I am touched beyond words
and honored to be 'of' you
and with you

Though our future is shrinking
our eternity is growing
and my gratitude goes beyond even that

Though my other homes are far
our understanding remains arm in arm
memorized like the look in our eyes
when we must say goodbye

June 3, 2003

Oceanfront Cafe

Thierry, from Nice
is a player in the Venice cast of thousands

Too handsome at first fifty glances
he's redeemed finally
by a shadowy Moorish streak
that allows him to sit at your table
when he asks to

A delicacy of manner
no American can master
alerts you to his worthiness
his presence humble in an Eastern way –
your space is forever your space

He speaks of Bali, Australia, the Philippines
foreign places inhabit his cells
the world is round to him
he doesn't compare
Survival for him has been a clarity
he is his own stamp of approval

A week later he joins you again
his details are perfect
but he can't help it
ugliness would kill him
He tries, in talk, not to care about
the teeming, heaving angst of the world
but he knows too much
You want him to teach you not to care
He thinks he can
but you end up caring more

He's afraid you're reading his mind
You're not, you're just watching
his thoughts remain his

He's not diversion
but you don't think about him when he's gone
you forget the cafe for days

When you go back
he joins you again
in his blue jeans
The way he sits
the way he leans on an elbow
seem designed by you
Still he doesn't matter
and you wonder if he's everybody's design

He was born in Morocco
and his great grandmother
was black from Senegal
He touches your hand to make a point now
about hippies being inadvertent colonialists
or Bertolucci's clichés
he's becoming somebody
His disdain for ordinariness
is really not pride
more like hope

You wrote the character
but now you can't remember a thing
it's all new
He can say anything
because you've made it clear that
his space is forever his
You know that's why he sits with you

Winter 1987, Venice

Part of Me

part of me runs from you gasping
while another me climbs onto your lap for a story

part of me feels frozen in your yard like a snowman
another me is melting in your mouth

part of me disapproves of you like heroin
another me keeps you like a puppy

part of me is afraid of you like a car accident
part of me searches for you like a rare species

Winter 1982, London

Intuition II

Intuition II sits at the dock like a black swan
anchored in Sag Harbor
like my siblings
Sleek smaller sailboats rest in the bay
they've worked hard to get here
so have I

and here we all float
between day and night
as locals talk about work and money
over dinner
and visitors stroll with ice cream cones

Rosie's still alive
Will she be in two weeks?
Euthanize her, my brother said matter-of-factly
No. Not my Rosie
not my brown-eyed life blood
not my best friend
not the girl who's walked
four thousand miles with me
not the one who spent a freezing winter
six months ago
in no man's land with me
not the one always willing, always ready
never tired, always smiling, always game

Rosie's very much alive
and will be long after she's gone
Right now she's surrounded by angels
she's breathing heavily
as we swim through this passage together
where everyone, yet no one really,
seems to understand
and strangers say better things to us
than family or friends

Don't die, Rosie
Stay with me, Rosie
You're my history, you're my health
you're the one who's seen me through
such a rocky time

Now I'm seeing you through your rocky time
I'm here, inches away, or closer
Let my hope be your Intuition II
to sail you through
Rosie Roo

My love is the wind in your sails

May 24, 2011, Sag Harbor, Long Island

The Forever Beach

This is the memory place
all souls are surfing here
the happy
the sad
the one constant through the years
now the lifetimes
It doesn't get old
but was never young

The every-which-way waves today
roll, tumble, play
pretty and fresh, the show must go on

Now Rosie's gone
I guess it's okay......somewhere
Maybe in south Texas
Here, she rushes into the surf
anyway
Gone or not
she's never gone
not my Rosebud, Rose-buddy
best friend ever

How many times did I say her name?
Now no answer

June 2, 2011, Coastguard Beach, Amagansett

Hat and Cane

Where are my tap shoes?
Where's my hat and cane?
I haven't any anger
I haven't any pain

Life is after all
just a merry merry dance
I'd tap right through the floor
if given half a chance

Spring 1983, London

Deciding Weather

Sometimes sadness is an open wound
but sometimes it's beautiful
like this row of lopsided empty benches
like English weather
Sometimes England's bleak, cruel like a skeleton
and sometimes its melancholia is musical
even on a freezing day in late July
Sometimes I feel a peace sweep over you in bed
and waft over to me
and we sleep like babies
Sometimes we're the same and understand a calm
but sometimes my wishes become targets
and your deeds arrows
Sometimes the smell of your skin
gives me a security I could never describe
despite our failures

Sometimes it's okay that nothing perfect lasts
but sometimes even the point of living
seems therapeutic
Sometimes death feels near
and I need drastic destiny
only to escape you
Sometimes it's sweet in its place,
like a cloudy day in summer
but sometimes it contradicts my soul
Sometimes failure seems like our last name
and all I want is another planet
Sometimes I can let it be
and half-know you with love
but sometimes the children we didn't have
grow older anyway
and watch us from trees
When I pack for Mars
I'm not sure I can leave you
but when I arrive at your door
I know I can't stay

July 28, 1982, Hampstead Heath, London

Last Laugh

You laughed at God
and it's your sin
Don't work it out with me
work it out with Him

June 1980, Venice

To Oma

Oh, I let you down
my rock
my well
my waterfall
always the source
the yes amidst endless no's

you had to die
without my hand to hold

Oceans away,
I didn't hear your call
lost in youth
deafened by love
I didn't hear your call

until too late
– you'd slipped away

Now I wish for another chance
to catch the very next plane
in time to say
I'm here, it's me
you know I'd never let you down

August 1974, Zaxos, Greece

Late Grape Sun

late grape sun
smooth almond eve
cool white sheets
to wear and sleep
painted blue into
landscape
can't escape
but village waits
gathering boats
and furling sails
buying fish its men-folk bring

village call – a bell, a smell
gossip collectors buy and sell

beautiful here
would you leave if...
beautiful here, glass of wine
and two ripe figs
Even time
has gone to town
only old ones linger now
more work to do
the goats, the cow

I'd almost live for you
but too old for love
you're twenty-one
nights alone
till you are young
village court you
late grape sun

August 18, 1974, Zaxos, Greece

The Cupping Room

old friends
in the amber light of the Cupping Room
gray rain in window
acoustic guitar

we've reached maturity
you and me, and the others
we are who we wanted to be
pens as swords
we meet each year
and compare past and future

this is the arrival
the summer of life
the fruit is on the tree
we must continue becoming
here, between young and old

because this poignancy of a perfect day
may not last
our vision may one day fade,
our will relax

or...
our vision may strengthen
and our will turn to crystal

April 7, 1988, NYC

Exhale Poem

Churning across the Continent
letter in hand
clutching his address like a full canteen
you reach for that far-off land...

The map is like your grandma,
too slow, but you must sit tight
sit until the 'pizza' signs
change to 'omelettes' in the night

And in that mountain valley
where liras turn to francs
too many short rides eat up your time
and fill your mouth with thanks

Then stumbling under eyelids
reddened by the strain
you point your thumb to a darkening sky
and demand it not to rain

As one more night subtracts itself
from the mileage on the map
you're jerked out of monotonous sleep
awakened with a slap...

The map goes in the garbage
the letter is reread,
and disbelief becomes relief
in the comfort of a bed

The morning shines in yellow
beneath the down-pulled shade
your face is washed and teeth are brushed
hotel bill quickly paid

A taxi takes you uphill
to the street spelled on the page;
the door is white, the number right,
you're just a knock away

"Come in." That's it, the same old voice
You walk into his eyes,
"You haven't changed." "Nor have you."
Just donned a new disguise

You share with him your journeys
and loves you've had since then
you swear you would have written
but you didn't have a pen

And round and round the words go
confessions flow in tears
until your arms absorb him
your one love through the years

"You'll never know," you tell him,
"how far you've made me go"
"Oh, no, my love," he shakes his head,
"it's you who'll never know."

But the chorus of the love song
is always just the same
He's once again the player
and the driver of the game

"A bit of a child you are," he speaks.
"And I, I am a man"
Without a why or a single reply,
you let him take command:

I have for you a ticket
on the Paris train at ten.....
Of course, of course I'll write to you
if I can find a pen"

"Oh God, oh Death," escapes your lip
"What's that?" says he, perplexed
"Oh never-mind – I'll be just fine
I know it's for the best"

Half his mouth turns upward
and he blinks you from his eye
"You've an hour and a half, now take your bath
or your hair will not be dry"

And one more time you're on your way
and he's where he fits best
inside your brain on the ten o'clock train
Amen. Farewell. God bless.

November 1972, train, Madrid to London

Two of You

Something about you
reminds me of him
and it hurts because he's dead
still I wait
even the pain I'd forget
just to see that man again

And though he's gone
in your voice he lives on –
And you,
you say you're a friend
then friend indeed
be my friend in need
this sorrow has to end

But to me somehow
you're more like a thief
like you're after my grief
and all of it isn't enough
I recall when you moved in with us
you fought him at every turn
you saw our love and watched with hate
'til you drove it all away

Now you wear his shirts
and mimic
gestures that he made
but you can't imitate his sweet eyes
or the love that crossed his face

So don't pretend
there's emotion to spend
or deception's some kind of game
In your two-faced charade
babe, two can play
I, too, am not the same

'Cause the day he died was my suicide
to me he meant the world –
so don't call me up and invite me to sup
Mister, I'm no longer that girl

March 14, 1982, London

Part II

Trouble

Oooh we got trouble
size thirty jeans
trouble at five foot eleven
trouble on that motorcycle
trouble in that kiss

Here comes trouble
with a capital T
Trouble
you're trouble
total trouble

I love trouble

May 22, 1989, Venice

Not Tellin'

"What're you doin' tonight?" he calls from Maui
"Cause I wondered if you could pick me up
at the airport"

And there he is, warm and blue
the man with the perfect act
throws his carry-ons in the back

"Where do y'wanna go?" I ask, "It's your night"
sideways smile
press down on the gas
wouldn't have to stop for anything again in my life

Later, the seven weeks are coughed up
my new 'plans' called out on his carpet
I sweat through a medley of ideas
"But I did cry myself to sleep last night"
"Any notion why?"
"Yeah...but I'm not gonna tell you"

Finally his arms
I take the deep breath
like I've been underwater for weeks
our kisses come from far away
and tentatively meet
unasked questions coat the lips

He sleeps, I watch
glance from dreams back to his face
he rolls over and holds me
"You sleep?"
"Uh-uh, didn't want to miss anything"

It's gonna be hard
but meanwhile it's easy

Summer 1989, Venice Beach

Raw

What is poetry, someone wanted to know
It's the mind translating the heart
it's the star-studded sky
as an answer to your loss
it's what exists in the vacuum
it's God when God's not home

it's tonight
it's the space
where my animals used to comfort me
it's the remaining time
of my father's life
it's sometimes all you have left

it's hot tears
it's after, and hopefully before
and it's never

It's mine, real, unreal
it's more than nothing, less than something
it's what's left,
but also a seed
it's hope

poetry is hope
a tiny whisper just asking
asking the huge night

the mind is soft, the heart swollen
did I hear an answer
or am I alone

I heard an answer

April 14, 2011, Wailua, Kaua'i

Can't Love

collage of emotion
slide show of eyes and faces,
memories of what men said
about their mothers
revealing their pain
letting you know

they can't love

can't love
what a notion
like can't eat, can't sleep, can't walk
what pain

where does it go then
the love?
where does it stop
where does it stay
where does it live
inside

where does it flow
where does it hide
where does it tell its secrets
where does it cry?

it cries all the time
cries and cries
and hides and shouts and screams inside
all the time
can't love is big
mean and wide
can't love is the rule
that can't be broke

but there's no escape
not a crack or leak
each seam is cemented
can't love just circles around
inside, up and back
in the brain, the arms
the hair, the mask

it lingers around,
a manifestation
afraid of its own shadow,
any liberation
a slide show of eyes and faces
a haunting inhabitation

can't love is contagious,
flows from one to another
till I too can't love
someone who can't love

September 6, 1990, Venice

Stuck on the Physical

He's gotta be beautiful
he's gotta have colors
beautiful eyes, and a feathery mind
Call it superficial, trite
Tell me I'm missing the boat

(If I'm missing the boat,
I already missed it
If I'm missing the boat,
I didn't want to go where that boat was going)

I'm not dreaming
these dreams come true
Anyway, I'm not on the straight and narrow
I'm hardly a citizen
barely on Earth
just traveling through, may not grow roots
may leave no trace
But it's a cool journey
from birth to death
and a blue planet to spend it on

And he's got to be beautiful

March 13, 1990, Venice

Fun Poem

fun

Winter 2012, Venice

Thanksgiving

Thanks and giving
A stranger in red pants traipses across the sand to me
Hi, how're you doin', got any reefer, what's your name?
I'm really happy to be by myself right now.
Oh, me too, he says,
and meanders off

Thanks and giving
I blow my nose after tearful holiday sentiment
Planning our first Thanksgiving together
there had to be a teardrop somewhere
If you're not ready by four-thirty, I'm going without you
he said
Can't you say it in a nicer way?
Yeah, I can, but I'm still gonna leave at four-thirty
no matter what
Well fine – maybe I won't go
You don't have to go if you don't want to

And there we are in the holiday snit
I thought we'd hurdled

The stranger in red pants,
a man with nothing to get ready for
at four-thirty
sifts through a trashcan and then another

I cry again
I came here to give thanks
and end up in tears

In four hours,
if I'm ready in time
we'll be raising our glasses
in a circle of family love
Thou preparest a table before us
I wonder if I give enough
– how to give more

And the stranger in the red pants
is gone

November 27, 1997, Venice Beach

The Madman

done
empty in aftermath
a year after greed in love
last year's great temptation now tombed as the stones
on which the town's idiot paces back and forth
back and forth
back and forth
pacing upon hours where answers once lay
his barless jail cell

I see you, Madman,
exactly as you were then
when I took notice of each stone's unique shape
Behind us in your reserved corner
you marched the months away
despite what we called love
waiting below our stomachs
to scream in defiance of you

You slept on those stones
under the cart of old fruit
you tried to sell
to no one
He's not crazy, the white-haired fisherman said,
he only has *psixi-pathos,* soul disease

But that was later
when I was mad too
just too young to pace
that was after
the night and day eyes of the fisherman's son
had become my own asylum
after he'd said all he could
without words
and I'd swum through the swells
a fish in his school
learning only awe

after he'd moved on,
returned,
moved on,
and returned again
only to show me his new pupil

then it no longer mattered
who haunted who
or feelings still stabbing

I wonder when the madman surrendered

July 19, 1975, Zaxos, Greece

Safe

We walked a hundred miles
but tonight you're on a bus
going home

We all went kind of crazy at the end;
ate for days when we came out
I went blank, knew we'd never kiss, and kept eating
you became smaller somehow and younger
and tried to fade into the city
but your jungle arms and legs
showed through
the new clothes

It was you
who got me through
I would've turned back
had you not been there
I should've told you
about the strength you gave me,
just being there
after I failed myself
and lay crying in the rain
on the jungle floor

I didn't mind your youth
because your hands made things
your muscles were bone
and your eyes were mine
You never kissed me
or hurt my feelings
you were kind, separate, helping,
with strength to spare

So many times I caught your eye
when we stopped for breath, drank waterfalls,
and cleaned our feet
And when it got rough
like it had to, I called your name
Who knows what you thought
when you made space for me
to sleep beside you

Something hovering over us
kept us apart
like childhood
Sitting by the river we were shy
silent after the others had gone
and time just passed

Then the last night
you held me
or were you just cold
on the jungle floor

I can believe it's over
but not that you're gone
our good-bye was so pale
beside that flame
you so delicately ignored
for twenty-four days,
while your eyes
fell in love
My cold rainy nightmares
of lying alone on the jungle floor
don't stop
though we've been out ten days now
There's more paper and more food out here
but less power
less time loving
and less being safe
in the most dangerous way

June 13, 1985, San Jose, Costa Rica

Forever

Thinking of forever without you
wouldn't be easy,
so I don't
But now without you
is fine,
and probably will be
forever

June 20, 1980, Venice

Wee Hours

The wee hours, why do they call them wee
when they drag by like freight trains
at 15 mph
as you wait to cross the tracks

No track to cross tonight
we crossed it on the phone at 7
"Why do we have to do this on a rainy night?"
I asked
It would crackle outside all night long
and I'd hear every drop
knowing you'd escaped to dreams

My ceiling sprang a leak beside my bed
Chinese water torture, drumming into a pot
I want to call the landlord, then you
then the landlord, then you
to a dreary tune

My mind runs down your body
the you that was certain
the part that held
The rest of you wavered,
and I'm not sure I cared
but I never questioned our oasis

You weren't everything
but you were a lot
and I learned why people settle
I saw us as comfort, not compromise

You were family
we shared food and time
never talked of tomorrow
I never saw the need
Until it arrived, like El Niño
crying through the roof
dripping into the skylight
wringing out the night

Now tomorrow's here and we're not
our todays are yesterdays
and even the huge wee hours
disappear down the track
The clanging bell stops
and that black and white arm
no longer blocks the road
But I just sit there
the way ahead lies empty
and I just want to go back

February 22, 1998, Venice Beach

Captain Paradise

Captain Paradise said it was going to be a good flight.
I had three seats
The sky stayed cloudy blue
till we saw the sunset island mist
then we landed early

For no reason
my rental car was upgraded to a four-wheel drive
Took a wrong turn out of the airport
and wound up on a windy, rocky beach
and gave my thanks to a zillion stars

Followed Suzi's directions to her new house
I had no plans and the address of a hostel
Stay here, she said
Roosters and birds in ridiculous profusion
bombarded my sleep at two a.m.
and continued for....the next two weeks
You'll get used to it, said Suz

Daybreak was a 360 degree tapestry
of flowering greenery
and mist-draped peaks

Ducky and Blondie
appeared at the back fence
for their daily carrots
and a brown chameleon
scrambled up a papaya tree
Molded its body around a green fruit
then changed color to match it
Suzi picked some Japanese eggplant
to compliment my veggie theme
and we were launched on a fortnight
of clean eatin'
Veggies morning, noon and night was how it went
we shopped and chopped, foraged and grazed
and felt so well

Island life – hot and humid
sun and rain taking turns in the sky
sparkling blue swims and stony, muddy hikes
long drives and long beaches
gentle isle of lush aloha
"It's all good" never seemed truer

Two weeks were just too short
Is there a bigger case for aloha (meaning 'love')?

Life itself was feeling short
short on purity, cleanliness, kindness, openness
and trust in goodness
Why would I not choose to live
in the best place I could find?

The answer was all around
There were just enough days left
to change the course of my life
every whisper of wind said yes
I started looking around....
as my final days diminished
I stayed simple – what would be would be

Then, boom, found it
the place I needed
a silver ring with a blue heart was on its back porch
I was sure
Later that day
I found a carved stone heart at the beach,
that said 'love' on the back
I signed the contract and bought the house

Tonight I'm flying away
but not for long
and I have three seats

May 7, 2003, in flight, Kaua'i to LA

Beauty

Sweeping beauty
so stunning
better, purer
than anything anywhere ever
clean and deep
as burning tears

but I told the night
I wouldn't gape in awe
told God I had no reason to cry
yet emotion wells up

Sweeping beauty
the wind works the sky
and fairytale clouds
distract from emotion
black palm fronds
swish across the rainbow around the moon
and the rush of ocean wind
rocks me
in the arms of beauty

March 5, 2017, Kaua'i

Su Casa es Su Casa

When we were together
I never wrote anything
was content

I thought of describing the storybook views
out your storybook windows
the pastel colors of nearby houses
They deserved description
like a beautiful woman in a flowered dress

We were beautiful, too
but feared big love
never lost ourselves in each other's eyes
no one would die for this

Now the story continues without me
and the part of me
that wanted to love you
write you and live your dream
meanders invisible down that street

The part of you I dug
breaks my heart
while the part that's for the birds
sets me free

So I'll watch my new life now like a movie
see what happens
but, shucks, here I am writing about lost love
while my own precious life I so cherish
feels like a consolation prize

February 22, 1998, Venice Beach

Place in Time

It was wrong from the start, a birthday bust
we snubbed the big three: should, ought and must
we found conversation, we welcomed lust
but our days were numbered, a limited trust

There was elbow room and space to play
moonbath night and sunblock day
through uncharted months we created a way
adrift, a laugh, a wave, a lei

Soul to soul it was an even score
sing-song harmony hinted at more
but could it be love forevermore?
not with Tick-Tock tappin' on the door

Yes, time was flying, as time will
time, the challenger, wouldn't sit still
it made monkey faces and jeered until
it ran out completely for Jack and Jill

Not to be confused with Romeo and Juliet
not the great pang that drives the great poet
a little yin, a little yang was more how we knew it
and you couldn't say we failed or that we blew it

'Cause we were kind and true, best of friends
we were silky and smooth in our midnight trends
we ate and drank and said our amens
it was an easy trail from beginning to end

But we knew from the start the math was wrong
we might write the lyrics, never the song
so in our past is where we'll belong
and Time, the master, marches along

October 20, 1997, Venice Beach

Hanama'ulu Beach

Mental free-fall
studying a blue sky
Hawaiian Airlines jet crosses the screen
I want every single answer
today
but no one to ask
my questions to

I want time to move
and it to stay still
I want everything
but most I want to feel right in my life
to know
but I never will

Can I ever be fearless again
after my fall?
Is this what scares us
takes away our stripes?
please don't take my stripes
I'm just a little scaredy-cat
on crutches
de-clawed
hoarding my invalid hours
like a savings account
to spend the wisdom later

Right now I want to be everywhere
including here
but how do you leave a place
when you already want to return?
Another Hawaiian Airlines jet streams away

I have no pride, dream or ambition
no one to ask
my questions to
just my broken dance
Little waves break at Hanama'ulu Beach
my broken leg rests in the open window frame
of this trusty car
I stare at this ironwood tree
soft piney green against the blue sky

the tree is dancing
joyous despite dead branches
glad to be alive

April 8, 2010, Hanama'ulu Beach

Calling All Cupids

I'm calling on every cupid
every star
every twinkly thing out there
stop what's happening
turn it around
bring us to our senses
use your magic

words got in the way
we got in the way
our sentences became nets
we got caught
we thrashed
couldn't get out

beam us, redeem us
find us
free us
put our hands back together
put our lips back together

February 3, 1990, Venice Beach

Don't Leave

Daddy don't leave me
there's no world without you

life-long friend
don't come to the end

leaving dark space
where the jokes never ceased
where your twinkle
was in my eye too
our history the same
our blood ran warm
we always were just the way we were

You're the pillar and the post, Dad
you started it
and somehow stayed strong
always answered the phone
always met the train
always put up the Christmas tree

Always there, Dad
always you
through the best and toughest times

Don't ever leave, Dad
please stay

November 17, 2015, Greenport, Long Island

The Road of Strangeness

Don't know how
I got so far down this road of strangeness
not sure where I missed the turn

not sure how to find my way
is it chemical or alchemical
is it a map I need, a hand, a surrender?

my humor is out of reach
it's awkward without it

yet I know dying people
who are still funny

my funny is lost
with my cat and darling dog
and Handsome the rooster
who lived in the mango tree

the house is a shell without them
life half full

I gave up everything
thinking I didn't have what I needed
sacrificed what I loved most
not realizing it was my world

I thought I could go back
and hold hands with the past
so I left everything
and re-traced the decades
almost back to birth

when I got there, I was nowhere
not even close
to the family I went to see
and lost the family that was real
there for me
that looked to me
each morning for love and food
that shared our home
that meowed and crowed and wagged its tail

nostalgia is where I live now
where the road has led

I could write uplifting twists
of hope and promise
but this place isn't like that

all the fantasy I built
has crumbled
and I must start over

but not today
today I'm still on that road
just walking
shrugging
carrying nothing

traveling light isn't what it was
it was once an art form
now it's an echo, an effort
but I do see a bridge
in the distance

that's what I tell myself
when my feet are sore,
my throat dry, my story dull
this isn't who I've become
it's just the road of strangeness

April 14, 2011, Wailua, Kaua'i

What Luck

And then I think of my magical dad
I could never explain
All I can do is try to be
like he was

like he still is

And the greatest tragedy of my small life
is that I couldn't have more of his time
But the greatest honor and prize
has been the miracle
that of all the people in the world
that could have shown me
how to simply live
I got someone who really knew how

September 17, 2014, Kaua'i

Open Road

I'm 62 years old
I have passed the early part of life
I know fear
        it's accessible
        friendly, a schmoozer, even a flirt
but it's a distraction
        a dangerous game, like gambling
        must be denounced
        all roads to it blocked

because the open road beckons
        though you see people getting off at exits
        or even turning back

But that's okay
a life is given to each
        to spend as they choose
        or as they must
no comparisons need be made

The open road isn't really about courage
        it's easier than that
it's more like letting up, or letting go
maybe changing one's commitment
        in the deepest sense
        or finding a deeper commitment
        or maybe one not as deep

Taking yourself by the shoulders
        for a gentle shake
        getting the chinks out of the armor
        created by the years

July 4, 2012, Princeville, Kaua'i

Over Here

I hardly exist
I'm not there
just h-e-r-e
in this glass bubble
not contaminated

not in IT

I'm out here
with the spirits and trees
where the dogs smile
the fish blink
and the boulders bear witness

no watch, no pot, no church,
no hairdresser, no hatred, no piercings,
no doctor, no stocks, no burn-out,
no meat, no violence, no booze,
no nine-to-five, no sunglasses, no shrink,
no arguments, no GMO, no new car,
no messed-up spine, no power bar,
no frowns, no brats, no pills,
no vaccines, no bottled water,
no blame, no waste

I'm not t-h-e-r-e
I'm here

August 2, 2014, Marina del Rey

What's Left

Poetry is what's left when you have nothing
it's the reminder
that you have no idea what 'nothing' is
you have everything

we know that
but it doesn't help tonight

nothing can help
when your father tells you
he feels death coming

poetry is all you've got

April 14, 2011, Wailua, Kaua'i

Pillow Talk

Pushing death away
that's what artists are doing
at four a.m.
making space
for life

staring death in the face
not backing down
dancing around its implications
deciding to live
volunteering for the mystery

Sometimes it's a victory
a glorious yes
That's art
Sometimes a tragic shrug
almost a no
That's art

but the willingness
is electricity
transforming to power
songs of nothing
or descriptions of vagueness
the pen racing away
silly with fatigue and delirium

Miser of words and clocks,
the hour belongs only to me
and those constellations usually not seen
The page grows shorter
then morning light sneaks in
and the cat yawns,
"Oh God, another poet"

September 17, 2014, Kaua'i

Ready or Not

There's one piece to this whole thing
that I can't fathom
one part that doesn't fit
one stone unturned

That stone is...
the rest of Dad's life
the part he didn't live
He had more miles
wasn't there yet
and everyone knew
dying wasn't his intention that day

That's where I falter
Is death always like that?
snatching you?
I thought we'd be offered
the opportunity to surrender
at some point
but Dad never did

morphine snatched him
he died fighting for life

May 30, 2017, Peter's Green, Sag Harbor

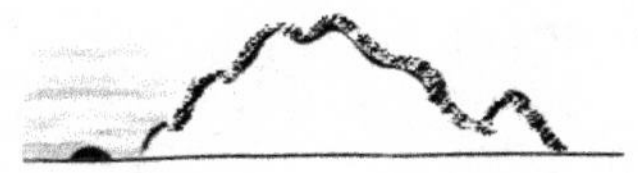

Gray Day

The day's as gray as his eyes
the bay as still as his bones
and free-floating geese
ask why I sit in the reeds
on this old beached boat with no sail

in Dad's brown sweater
I blend right in
at one with the earth
as he was

humming in the background
you hear the town
shoppers, drivers, errands, groceries
death blends right in
just on the other side
over the hill

And it's okay
until I see that cutest smile
forever gone
with the visionary gaze

Then it's not okay
and a million tears
drench Dad's sweater

May 30, 2017, Peter's Green, Sag Harbor

The House

I won't go look in the windows
I won't even go up on the porch
I'll stand here down the street
and gaze

as if you were there

time continues
no matter what
no matter how much I loved you
no matter how much I blew it

in the end
all of our forgiveness
is what remains

and the house

December 24, 2017, walking in Greenport

To Leslie I

All of humanity
is the shoulder I cry on
everyone understands this grief

all of humanity feels my loss
as their own

the loss of family
old, young, crazy, or sane
is a forever subtraction
eternal echo
never to subside

one of us has departed
never to return
part of me
is gone

June 8, 2017, Northern California

Spirits aren't Spooky

The spirits aren't spooky
it's spookier down here
Here's where the goblins
and gluttons abide and thrive
Here, greedsters and needsters
the thankless and the vain
uncaring, entitled
the carnivores and the strange

it's mean, riotously awful
in the grander scheme
Give and forgive
to your heart's exhaustion
but always count your change

Trust and love? I s'pose...
but the spirits
have their fingers crossed
for us down here
where Halloween is every day
So say your prayers loud and clear
your only escape, folks
is up there

December 26, 2017, Sag Harbor, Long Island

In the Wake

This flight to Hawai'i
was so gloriously exciting
back when

Island life reached for me
ecstatically
I was smitten with luck and blessings
"I'm jealous of myself,"
I used to say

before the commuting to New York
dragging the wintry baggage
burdened by disgruntled family
and the weight of my commitment

At least I loved
gave my all

But Hawai'i grew farther out to sea
more and more remote
harder to return to
Workload tarnished the tropical shine,
spread-sheets replaced watercolor paintings

"But it's Hawai'i, it's Hawai'i..."
I'd remind myself
while the red-eyes and rental cars
unforgettable remarks
and cash outlay
had to be ignored
the way you keep walking with a blister
on a long hike

"It's family, it's love,"
I'd remind myself
while plane rides to Paradise
became just chunks of nine-hour suspension
between sky and sea

I never returned to Hawai'i empty-hearted though
just uncertain where home was...

Now Hawai'i's home again
family love at rest
in eternity

fatigue and wear may have eclipsed
the novelty and intrigue
but there's no question about Hawai'i's glory
just some about my own

June 15, 2017, in flight to Kaua'i,
days after Dad and Leslie passed

Nature's Urge

What is this life experience all about?
We're born
we're here
we grow
and years pass
we try out these bodies at various stages
we roll along

It's easy to get rusty or crabby
hesitant
or unforgiving
Easy to back down
get tired of the fight
the fight to live

But then there's a happy dog
a fluffy cat
a swaying poppy
on a clean waft of winter
there's youth and hope
and dignity
there's the graceful parade
of the future
there are wide white smiles
and most of all there's loving kindness
and all of nature's urge to
live

March 1, 2013, Santa Monica

Gotta Be

I am a goddess
I don't doubt myself
I take divine instruction
the wind is my messenger
the water is my cleanser
the night is my shelter
the day is my spear

My hands are open
my heart is good
Fear is my teacher
opening every new door
Imperfection is my sister, my twin
I learn to understand her
and worship her honesty

I have no past
I walk on new ground every day
clean air is my food, showered from heaven
I touch you with my eyes
kindness is a language here
silence goes a long way
'alone' is the answered prayer for silence

Autumn 2004, Kaua'i

Shut It

It's too bad
I have to regard my regards for you
    as an affliction
too bad I have to stop myself
from remembering funny things you said
    or those last few kisses
I congratulate myself now for disliking you
    and forget your mouth altogether

That mouth full of crazy sentences
    and sane kisses
    and those lips
    and your busy little teeth
Even in my dream you were munching a sandwich

You talk Walt Whitmans around my Walden Pond
Henry David Thoreaus around my Roget's Thesaurus
your ten-tiered phraseology
    thick with enticement like some gourmet deli
lingers around my brain
    like the smell of apple pie baking
    in some mom's oven
Weren't you noshing hot apple pie
    when we met?

I'd like to meet you again
and this time, when you open that mouth
even for a bite of pie
I'd say shut up
and the poetry would never start
and the turn of phrase would never turn to kisses
and I'd be sure like I was before
that no one in this town
knows how to snatch the whim from the breeze
or hold it, then spice it, then say it
Or knows how to hold my love and spice it
and actually say it
And I'd admit that art is obsolete
not optimistic in open hearts
and I wouldn't have to regard my regards for you
as an affliction

November 1, 1990, Venice Beach

To Leslie II

I'm sorry
my dear sister
that we couldn't go
hand in hand through life

But we always laughed
we looked for the laugh

We understood early
that our trails would rarely cross
but we reached across the chasm
always

And you once gave me a ruby ring
for reconnecting you
with Dad
it meant that much to you
you said

Now the ring means that much to me
as you did
dear one
who had it so tough
and could never get
the sympathy you needed
Instead we gave advice
that you hated
we didn't understand,
you said,
how hard it was for you

We didn't give up on you
but we couldn't help because
in the end
we really didn't understand

June 8, 2017, Northern California

I Will Not Pretend

I will not pretend
and I won't be quiet
I'll even suffer and cry
like a baby
who can't take it

Because maybe it's just too much
maybe they're all pretending
maybe the castle's made of paper
and the shriekers and haters
are the true and holy

I got in the cross-fire
now I'm doomed
knowing too much
seeing the lies
protecting the guilty –

while the accusing outliers
burn in bitterness
and grow old without us

December 26, 2017, Sag Harbor, Long Island

Romance

oh lovely romance
you do exist
oh reason to pour wine
into delicate Moroccan glasses
lighting candles in the midnight
lying in the dark beneath the magnolia tree

oh the whiff of you, romance
the hint, the scent,
lost in the jungle of years
oh the tease, even false,
I lift my glass
and savor the night again

the coy beginning
ridiculous odds
but thank you just the same
for the slightest glimmer
the gentlest implication
of being caught off guard
by someone else off guard
like scattered pick-up sticks
touching
by toss

April 5, 2013, Venice

About Death

Couldn't ask for a better spot
than a wooden seat in the reeds
beside a vast still bay
undisturbed
at the end of another flat-line day

When death comes, you just watch and wait
See what it will do to the lives left behind
It doesn't haunt, doesn't dance, doesn't even speak
but it jumps out of songs and thoughts
ruffles every memory
massages every heart

Mischievous
how it belittles reality
when it climbs on board your life
blinding you with love and emotion

Death carries beauty and poignancy
yet it's despised
It makes us feel love
yet we hate it
It brings everyone closer
yet we run from it
It's illusive
yet everywhere
It's subtle and invisible
yet sharper than knives and more valuable than money
It sings and cries and weeps and waits
but is as stealthy as the deepest night
It's the end of the spectrum
yet as common as breath
It's the final end of something huge
yet a new beginning
It's ever-present to all of us
yet always a stranger
It walks and stalks in total mystery
yet we have all our lives to study it

We get nowhere with death
it always wins
The only way is to meet it
with open heart
Reach out to it, say hello
and see what it is offering

May 30, 2017, Peter's Green, Sag Harbor

Little Kitty

There was a little kitty
he had a little flea
oops he had two
oops he had three

I started counting
four, oh no five!
no one could believe
this cat was still alive

We went on red alert
number six, number seven
we called the Pearly Gates
to book a spot in heaven

Flea number eight
flea number nine
I looked around the room
everyone was cryin'

The cat remained blasé
number ten, then eleven
the Pearly Gates called back
"no fleas allowed in heaven"

So we'd dial nine-one-one then
if we reached a baker's dozen
then came number twelve
and his jumpy little cousin

But I couldn't find another...
then the kitty leapt away
free forever of fleas
or free today anyway....

August 13, 2014, Venice

Cool Breeze

Mom's birthday
She'd have been ninety-four
And she got a present this week:
Dad
after their forty-eight–year separation

"Are you with Mom now?"
I asked the gray sky,
trying to peer through the clouds

"That's for me to know and for you to find out,"
answered Dad
as if nothing happened last week

That's my boy! There he is!

And today I saw them
strolling together in spirit
reunited

The upside of death
– you get to glide with the ghosts
as they buoy up the mortals below
helping us along
protecting and guiding

You get to explore with them
that vastness above the clouds
mingle with the all-seeing and invisible
finding out, at last what it's all about

The breeze gets cooler
here by the bay
I don Dad's warm sweater
he won't be needing it now

May 31, 2017, North Haven Bay Beach

Harvest Poem

this moment
clean and refined
courses and horses at an even trot

but I can't hold or harvest it
like waves or the wind
it can't be contained

generosity's my only recourse
acknowledging
the alchemy of luck
still, it can't last...

memories will though
memories of perfection
the lemon tree,
the white cat
swishing through the bounty,
the beauty

And I can hold
my breath
during birdsong
can sleep in the afternoons
then wake and gaze around,
never grasping such completion
wanting to even the score
yet always coming out ahead

November 1, 2019, Kaua'i

Smile

So smile like you're the sun
give because it moves you
receive as if you're the giver
forgive as if you're the receiver
accept life's curve balls
like they make any sense

and handle the chaos
like a lousy hand in poker
it's just a round in the game
next hand will be different

September 21, 2017, Kaua'i

School of Life

When my ancient father told me
he was in love with life
I really didn't know what he meant
it was like yogic 'truth'
a little vague for a mid-lifer
halfway up an unbalanced ladder

Love, life, truth?
How about someone to hold the ladder?

I didn't realize Dad has holding it
by letting me in on the secret
like 'There is no spoon'

It sounded simple
like 'Just read the book'
but the trick to it, the keys, the manual
were nowhere to be found
on my little chessboard
The only hints were Dad's eyes
and how he soared above

That was my gospel, right there
but I didn't know it
His survival depended on it, though
while mine was an advanced level Sudoku game
of planes and careers and loan balances

He never gave me what I thought I needed
never held the damn ladder
but he taught me
every minute
how to love life
And I finally actually got it
I read the book

He loved me with his time
he loved me with his eyes
he loved me with his quiet heart
the heart of a teacher
And I got up the ladder all by myself

November 17, 2019, Kaua'i

End 1

Part III

*– a wee gifty for your next Halloween invitation
(just keep my name attached please!)*

Hallow! - *by W. M. Raebeck*

*Come good spooks, bad spooks, fat ghosts, thin ghosts,
the Father, Son, and the Holy one
Come harlots, starlets, Rhetts and Scarlets,
queens and drag queens,
the raging and the aging
big and hairy or not-so-scary
healthniks, sickniks, nags and bitches
goblins, I-got-a-problems, and comfortably riches
Come ye mediocre, ye very bourgeois
ye not-so-fabulous, ye better-by-far
Come Born Again, Dead Again – we'll all be united
police, whores, and bigots – we'll all get excited
Bring poisons and potions for a toxic treat
intense and bad, we are what we eat!
Come sergeants, lieutenants, gaffers and grips,
pilots, shrinking violets, and on-a-bad-trips
Welcome nerds and absurds, pirates and pervs
in-laws and out-laws for your just desserts*

radically mundane or way insane,
crazed and DOA's
those fallen-out-of-love
or all of the above

Misfits, half-wits, crims and crumbs
toothless, ruthless, dims and dumbs
ye maladjusted or not-to-be-trusted
cheaters, wife-beaters, y'red meat eaters
Got nowhere to run? Nowhere to hide?
Step out of limbo, to the West Side
Come wiggy and strange, doomed and done-for
to ____party address here____ *just once more*
Come *just-as-you-feared: dangerously weird*
helpless and hopeless, confined to a bed
nervous, neurotic, already pronounced dead
those without essence, gameshow contestants
crowned ones, robed ones, them covered in jewels
in flocks or just socks, them landed fools
The spirits and the spirited are all invited;
the half-dead and the stone-dead will be re-ignited
Come *all and sundry – Saturdy, not Sundy*
all are accepted, not just Eerie and Gory
everyone's invited, even Same Ol' Story!
But rsvp, all y'sweaty scammers
for once in y'life, at least fake s'manners

October 1992, Venice

End II

If you enjoyed 'Silence of Islands,'
pop a review onto Amazon.
Reviews are the gifts that keep on giving,
and they let authors know your thoughts.

Visit 'WendyRaebeck.com'
to be on my email list
regarding new releases and promotions.

To read more of my books,
check out the next page.
(Each book is different!)

Other W. M. Raebeck Books

"I Did Inhale — Memoir of a Hippie Chick"

"Stars in Our Eyes" — true stories

"Expedition Costa Rica"

"Some Swamis are Fat"
(currently under pen-name Ava Greene)

all in print and ebook
available everywhere

— ***audio coming soon*** —

Next Book:

"Nicaragua Story —
Back Roads of the Contra War"
(my email list gets advance notice)

7-13-20

CPSIA information can be obtained
at www.ICGtesting.com
Printed in the USA
JSHW011032010820
7063JS00001BA/25

9 781938 69115